Greek Mythology

The Complete Guide to Greek Gods & Goddesses, Monsters, Heroes, and the Best Mythological Tales!

Table of Contents

Introduction

Thank you for taking the time to pick up this book about Greek mythology!

In the following chapters, you will learn about the different Greek gods, deities, monsters, and heroes that are talked about in mythology. You will discover the different bloodlines and family trees of both the Olympian gods, as well as the Titans.

Included, are some of the most famous and interesting mythological tales, such as how the universe came to be, Heracles' (Hercules) 12 labors, and the great war between the Olympians and the Titans.

Tales of Greek mythology have been passed down for thousands of years, and have gone on to have a great impact on Western society. These stories are the inspiration for many poems, books, movies, and television shows. This book aims to provide you with a greater understanding of these incredible stories, and why they are so powerful and intriguing!

Once again, thanks for choosing this book, I hope you enjoy it!

Chapter 1: What is Greek mythology?

Greek mythology encompasses stories, teachings and myths surrounding Greek gods, heroes, creatures, practices, and rituals. It is considered to be part of the religion being followed in Ancient Greece.

Greek mythology attempts to explain several concepts, such as the origin of our world, lives of the various gods, goddesses and heroes, and the existence of mythical creatures. While it is possible to gather knowledge about Greek myths from literary sources like Homer's *Odyssey* and *Iliad*, you can also find inscriptions about these myths and stories in ancient vase paintings and other artifacts. In other words, both literary works and archaeological evidence serve as sources of Greek mythology.

Homer's poems deal at length about the Trojan War and its impact. *Works and Days* and *Theogony* are poems, which deal with concepts such as how the world came into existence, rule of the Gods, succession and rule by the humans, how the human woes came into existence and also how various rituals and practices came to be. Literatures that surround Greek myths are collectively referred to as Ancient Greek Literature.

The discoveries of both the Mycenaean and Minoan civilizations were instrumental in gaining an insight into the Greek culture and mythology. Archaeological evidence sheds light on the details of various Greek gods and goddesses and heroes. Several artifacts depict famous Greek heroes, gods and myths. Designs on pots depict various scenes from the adventures of Heracles, the Trojan cycle, and many other mythological tales.

Greek mythology was, and still is, a source of inspiration for several poets, writers and artists. To this day it is the basis for many films, books and television shows. In the following chapters, you will discover some of the most fascinating of these Greek mythology tales, and learn a little more about the different characters involved!

Chapter 2: Primordial Deities

Greek mythology commences with the primordial deities. These deities were the first beings who came into existence in this world. The union of some of these deities resulted in the birth of the gods and goddesses.

Aether
Aether was the god of light and upper atmosphere. His element was wedged between the heaven and the air encompassing the realm of mankind.

Ananke
Ananke represents inevitability, necessity and compulsion. She was the mate of Chronos. Ananke is depicted as a serpentine circling the entire world. She was regarded as an incorporeal.

Chaos
Chaos was the god of the lower atmosphere. In other words, she was the bridge between Aether and earth's landmass. Certain myths go on to describe Chaos as void.

Chronos
Chronos was the symbol of time. Chronos was also an incorporeal like Ananke, who was his mate. He was believed to have three hands and a serpentine tail. Myths say that he circled the world too, entwined with his mate.

Erebrus
Erebrus was the god of darkness. He found his way into hollow earth and found shelter in the underworld.

Eros

Eros was the god of generation and the god of love. He was the son of Ares and Aphrodite. Eros was believed to be the reason why the world was able to procreate and exist.

Gaea

Gaea was the goddess of earth or Mother Earth. She was one of the deities, who emerged at the time of genesis of this universe. She was responsible for laying the foundation of the universe.

Hemera

Hemera was the goddess of the day. Her mother, Nyx, is the goddess of the night.

Hydros

Hydros was the symbol of the element of water. His association with earth led to the formation of the first mud.

Ourea

Ourea was regarded as the god of the mountains.

Nyx

As already mentioned, Nyx was the goddess of the night. Several myths also indicate that she was the consort of Erebrus.

Pontus

Pontus was the god of the sea. He is regarded as the father of fishes and other sea creatures.

Tartarus

Tartarus was regarded as the god of the darkest and deepest segment in the underworld. Several stories indicate that he was the lord of the pit to which the Titans were condemned to, after losing the war against the Olympians.

Thalassa

Thalassa also represented the sea. She was born by the union of Hemera and Aether. She was also the consort of Pontus.

Uranus

Uranus was the god of the heavens. He is the father of the Titans. His consort was none other than Mother Earth, Gaea.

Chapter 3: Olympian Gods

Olympian Gods are regarded as the primary deities in Greek mythology. These gods are referred to as "Olympian Gods" because they resided on Mount Olympus. Let us now look at the Olympian gods and goddesses.

Aphrodite

Aphrodite was regarded as the goddess of love, desire and beauty. She was extremely beautiful, which drew the attention of many. Added to her natural beauty and charm, she also possessed a magical girdle. This was responsible for invoking desire in many.

There are a couple of stories, which deal with the birth of Aphrodite. There is one version, which states that she is the daughter of Zeus and Dione. There is another version however, which suggests that Aphrodite was born from the sea when Cronus castrated Uranus.

She was the wife of Hephaestus. Several theories suggest that she had an affair with Ares, the god of war, who was also her brother. Myrtle was Aphrodite's holy tree, while sparrow, swan, and dove were her holy birds.

Apollo

Apollo was born from the union of Zeus and Leto. Artemis was his twin sister. His mother was a Titan goddess. She was banished from the island, when Zeus' wife, Hera, found that she was carrying Zeus' child. Leto moved to the island of Delos, where she gave birth to Artemis first. A day later, Apollo was born, with the help of the other inhabitants of the island.

Apollo was the god of healing, truth, music and light. Several theories indicate that mankind was gifted with science by Apollo. It is also believed that he used to send out his four-horsed chariot every day, to move the sun across the sky and mark the beginning of a day.

Apollo was regarded as an Oracular god and was worshipped as a prophetic deity in the Oracle in Delphi. Through his priestess, Pythia, worshippers who visited the Oracle came to ask about their future.

Several stories indicate how he used his healing powers, time and time again, to heal several people. At the same time, it is also said that Apollo was capable of bringing about diseases and plagues by using his arrows.

Laurel was the holy tree of Apollo, while the dolphin was his holy animal.

Ares

Ares was the god of war. His parents were Zeus and Hera. Ares was famous for his rage and his unruly acts during a war. Owing to his violent nature, both his parents disliked him. Theories suggest that Ares was supporting the Trojans during the Trojan War. However, he ended up losing the war because of his failure to plan strategically. This shortcoming led to his defeat in many wars.

As already mentioned, he had an affair with Aphrodite, his sister. It was said that when her husband, Hephaestus, found out about them, he came up with a plan to humiliate the two of them in front of the other gods.

Aphrodite and Ares gave birth to eight children. Eros, the god of love, is the most famous of their children.

Stories suggest that warriors used to worship Ares and offer him their sacrifices before going into war.

It is said that every time Ares went to war, he was accompanied by his two companions, Deimos (terror) and Phobos (fear). Phobos and Deimos are the children of Ares and Aphrodite. It is also said that, Eris, the goddess of discord, who was also the sister of Deimos and Phobos, accompanied Ares sometimes during war.

Artemis

Artemis was regarded as the goddess of chastity, moon, virginity, natural environment, and the hunt. As already mentioned, she is the daughter of Leto and Zeus and had a twin brother, Apollo.

Leto had given birth to Artemis, during her stay in the island of Delos. Because Artemis assisted Leto in giving birth to Apollo the day after she was born, she is regarded as the protector/guardian of labor and childbirth. She requested Zeus to grant her eternal chastity and virginity, to which he obliged. It is said that Artemis never gave into the flowery words and deeds of men, who could have been her potential lovers. Myths indicate that she spent her life hunting and living with nature. Several stories indicate that she was the protector of nature and all animals. It is also said that she spent time herding animals and practicing agriculture.

While she never had companions or lovers, certain myths indicate that she had fallen in love with Orion, who was her hunting companion.

Athena

Athena was regarded as the goddess of reason, intelligence, art, and literature. Her father was Zeus. The reason why Athena is different from the other children of Zeus is that she sprang to life from within Zeus. Myths state that Athena was born from the forehead of Zeus. According to these myths, as soon as she sprang to life from her father's forehead, she was fully grown and was wearing her armor.

Athena was famous for her strategic plans in the wake of a war. Tales also talk about her bravery and fierceness on the battlefield. Whenever it was felt that the peace of the State was at stake, she was the first person to go to war. She was regarded as the symbol of purity and wisdom. She was also regarded as the patron of agriculture, the city, and handicraft. It is said that Athena invented many things such as the pot, bridle, trumpet, flute, rake, plow, yoke, chariot, and ship.

Her holy tree was the olive. It is said that during a contest against Poseidon, Athena won over the Athenians by offering them the olive tree. This is why she is regarded as the goddess of Athens.

The holy bird of Athena was the owl.

Hades

Hades was the brother of Zeus and Poseidon, and was said to be the ruler of the underworld. When Zeus, Hades, and Poseidon overthrew the rule of Cronus, the brothers picked lots to decide who got to rule which part of the universe. Hades picked the underworld and that's how he became the god of the underworld and the ruler of the dead. It is said that Hades was always greedy and wanted to increase the number of his subjects.

Certain myths also indicate that Hades was also known as Plouton, and was regarded as the god of wealth. It is said that the Greeks were terrified of uttering the name of Hades, fearing that he might find them and take them to the underworld. Hence, they started calling him Plouton, which symbolizes the precious metals that are mined from the earth.

Hades' weapon was the pitchfork, which he used to create several earthquakes. It is said that he also possessed a helmet of invisibility. The Cyclopes had gifted Hades the invisibility helmet, for helping them out in the war against the Titans.

It is also said that Hades abducted Persephone and carried her to the underworld, where he married her.

Hephaestus

Hephaestus was regarded as the god of the blacksmiths, sculptors, metallurgy, fire and volcanoes. Archaeological and literary sources depict him with a pair of tongs, hammer, and an anvil.

The birth of Hephaestus is not clearly known since there are a couple of different theories surrounding his birth. One states that he is the son of Zeus and Hera, while the other suggests that Hera conceived Hephaestus by herself.

It is said that the reason why Hephaestus never grew up on Mount Olympus is because Hera threw him off the mountain when she found that he was crippled. Eurynome and Thetis rescued him from the ocean and raised him. There is another myth, which suggests that Hephaestus was thrown off the mountain by Zeus. This is because Hephaestus tried to protect his mother against the advances of Zeus.

The throw from the mountain added to the physical deformity of Hephaestus. He was raised in the island of Lemnos. As he grew up, he became a master in craftsmanship. He was later accepted by the other gods and he moved to Mount Olympus. He continued being a craftsman and took on the responsibility of forging armors, shields and all sorts of weapons for the gods. As mentioned previously, his wife was Aphrodite.

Hera

Hera was regarded as the patron of marriage as well as childbirth. She was not only the sister of Zeus, but was also his wife. Hera was raised by Oceanus and Tethys, who were Titans. She went on to become the savior for married women and often took special interest in safeguarding them. Her holy animals were the peacock and the cow.

It is said that her marriage to Zeus was built on nothing but lies and trickery. Myths state that Zeus courted her on multiple occasions, and that she had rejected his advances. Disappointed by her rejections, Zeus devised a plan to win her over. He took the form of a disheveled cuckoo and appeared in front of Hera. Having looked at the sad state of the bird, Hera felt sorry for it. She took the bird in her hands and placed it near her breasts to keep it warm. Zeus regained his human form at this juncture, which was something Hera did not see coming. Her momentary lapse was used by Zeus to his advantage and he raped her. To cover up this shameful act, Hera had no choice but to marry Zeus. This was just the beginning of a marriage filled with resentment, arguments, and clashes.

Zeus was infamous for treating the other gods in a harsh manner. Hera and the other gods thus had a common motive, which was to overthrow Zeus. As a result, they decided to revolt against him. Zeus was drugged by Hera and he was rendered unconscious. As soon as he lost his consciousness, he was bound to his chair by the other gods and Hera. However, nobody had a clue about what to do next with the unconscious Zeus and ended up arguing with each other. Amidst all this commotion, Briareus, who was in Zeus' debt, snuck in and set Zeus free.

When Zeus woke up and stood up, with his thunderbolt by his side, the other gods were seized by terror. They immediately fell to their knees and begged for his mercy and forgiveness. Zeus immediately went for Hera and seized her. He hung her up in the sky, using golden chains. She spent the entire night up in the sky, weeping from the pain of being bound by chains. The other gods were unable to do anything to relieve her from her shackles. Her constant weeping kept Zeus up at night. He promised to relieve her from the chains if she promised to never instigate a revolt against Zeus again. Having been left with no other choice, Hera promised to never rebel against him and she kept her word. However, she never missed an opportunity to voice her distaste about the infidelities of Zeus.

Hermes

Hermes was the god of commerce. He was the son of Zeus and Maia. He was famous for his cunningness as well as his swift action. These traits rendered him an efficient messenger for the gods. He was capable of travelling between the world of humans and gods effortlessly.

He was regarded as the protector of athletes, travelers, and thieves. Several stories also state that Hermes helped in guiding souls of the dead to reach the underworld and commence their afterlife there. There are several myths, which talk about Hermes fooling other gods many times!

It is said that when Hermes was a child, he had given his lyre to Apollo. After his birth, it is said that Hermes jumped from the crib, snatched Apollo's cattle and returned back to his crib and pretended as if nothing happened. When Apollo found out that it was Hermes behind the theft of his cattle, he dragged him before Zeus, seeking justice. However, Zeus found Hermes' act amusing and witty. As a result, he did not punish Hermes. To apologize for his act, Hermes handed over the lyre, which he invented, to Apollo.

Hestia

Hestia was regarded as the goddess of hearth, family, and domestic life. She symbolized the relationship that existed between many cities and colonies. Her brother was Zeus. Although she was an Olympian God by birth, Dionysus was responsible for stripping her of this status. It is said that Apollo and Poseidon made advances towards her and she thwarted them successfully. As a result of these experiences, she swore an oath to remain a virgin forever.

Poseidon

As mentioned previously, Poseidon was the brother of Zeus and Hades. When the brothers overthrew their father, they drew lots to decide who got to rule what. Poseidon drew the lot containing the sea and thus became the god of the sea. He was regarded as the protector of the ocean and all the aquatic creatures.

His wife was Amphitrite, who was a granddaughter of Oceanus, a Titan. Certain myths indicate that Poseidon truly desired to be with the daughter of Cronus and Rhea; Demeter. She set a task for Poseidon to create the most beautiful animal, with an intention to stall his advances. With a view to impress her and win her over, Poseidon is said to have created the world's first horse.

Poseidon's weapon was the trident. It is said that he was capable of creating earthquakes and shattering any object, with the help of his trident. Poseidon was regarded as the second most powerful god, the first one being Zeus. It is said that Poseidon was also greedy like his brother, Hades. This greediness often resulted in several conflicts between Poseidon and the other gods.

Zeus

While drawing lots with his brothers, Zeus picked the lot containing the sky. He ended up succeeding his father's throne and became the god of the sky and rain. He also went on to become the ruler of the other gods.

His weapon was the thunderbolt. Anybody who defied Zeus' authority, such as liars and oath breakers, were punished by Zeus using the thunderbolt. His marriage to Hera was a troubled one, as Hera was forever questioning his authority and voicing her disapproval of his many illicit affairs.

Myths state that he was considered as the god of all the natural phenomena associated with the sky, and was thus responsible for storms, tempests, rains, and darkness. With the help of his shield, Aegis, Zeus was able to conjure lightning, thunders and rain. He was responsible for bringing about changes in the seasons. He was also regarded as the regulator of time and was responsible for bringing about every day and night. He was even charged with the responsibility of upholding several institutions in the State. He was regarded as the protector of people, and also as the friend of Princes.

In his role as the ruler of the other gods, he ensured that the other gods and goddesses performed their duties properly. In case any of them breached their duties, Zeus punished them. He also provided the other gods and goddesses with timely counsel, to help them perform their duties.

Zeus was also the father of men. He was regarded as the paternal figure for all mortals, who would often come to him, seeking his counsel. Stories state that he showered all mankind with love and kindness and was fair to them. He rewarded those who were honest and truthful, while punishing those who followed the path of deceit and lies.

Chapter 4: Titan Gods

The Titans ranked second in the order of divinity, after the Primordial deities. However, their position was usurped by the Olympian gods, who defeated them in the battlefield. This chapter will help you gain an insight into the various Titan gods.

Asteria

Asteria's parents were Coeus and Phoebe. Her sister was Leto. We already know that Leto was the mother of Apollo and Artemis, the Olympian gods. Perses, who was also a Titan, was her husband and her daughter was Hecate. She was regarded as the goddess of nocturnal oracles and shooting stars.

Certain myths indicate that Zeus was in pursuit of Asteria. To escape his advances, she transformed herself into a quail. Certain myths also indicate that she transformed herself later into Ortygia, which was known as the quail island. This island was linked to the island of Delos later.

Astraeus

Astraeus was regarded as the god of the dusk as well as the winds. His parents were also Titan gods, Eurybia and Crius. He married Eos, who was regarded as the goddess of the dawn. It is said that he was the father of the five Astra Planeta (also known as wandering stars or planets) and the four Anemoi (winds).

Atlas

Atlas was the son of Iapetus and Clymene. He was regarded as the god of navigation and astronomy. His brothers were Prometheus, Menoetius, and Epimetheus. It is said that when the war between the Olympian gods and the Titan gods broke out, Menoetius and Atlas had sided with the Titans and fought for them. On the other hand, Epimetheus and Prometheus sided with the Olympian gods and fought for them. It is said that Atlas led the Titans in the war. Once the Olympian gods won the war, Zeus decided to punish Atlas and condemned him to stand on the western front of the Gaea for all eternity. He was also condemned by Zeus to forever carry Uranus on his shoulders. There is a common misconception that Atlas is carrying the earth on his shoulders. However, Atlas was carrying Uranus on his shoulders.

He was married to his sister Phoebe, and had a lot of children with her, namely; Pleiades, Hyades, Hesperides, Hyas, Calypso, Dione, and Maera.

Clymene

Clymene was regarded as the goddess of renown, fame, and infamy. She was the daughter of the Titans, Tethys and Oceanus. Her husband was Iapteus. She had four sons; Prometheus, Atlas, Menoetius, and Epimetheus. Certain stories also indicate that she was a consort of Helios and their son was Phaeton.

Coeus

The parents of Coeus were Uranus and Gaea. He was the Titan god, who was responsible for invoking curiosity and inquisitiveness in mankind.

Coeus had three brothers, Crius, Iapetus, and Hyperion. The four brothers were responsible for acting as the four pillars, which held the earth and heavens apart. Coeus symbolized the pillar in the North. It is said that he and his brothers played an important role in overthrowing the rule of Uranus, their father.

He had two children, Asteria and Leto. When the war erupted between the Titans and the Olympians, he tried as much as possible to stop Zeus and the other Olympians. As a result, once the war was over, he was banished to the underworld where he spent the rest of his life. He attempted to break his chains and escape the underworld once. However, his escape attempt was foiled when he was stopped by the underworld's guardian, Cerberus.

Crius

Crius was the son of Gaea and Uranus. His wife was Eurybia, who was the daughter of Gaea and Pontus. Perses, Astraeus, and Pallas were his children.

As mentioned previously, Crius was one of the pillars of the world. He symbolized the pillar in the South. Crius fought alongside the other Titan gods during the war. As a result, he was also banished to spend the rest of his life in the underworld.

Cronus

Cronus was also the son of Uranus. It is said that he had castrated his father and assumed his throne. He was married to Rhea. Their children were the first Olympian gods.

Because he had usurped his father's throne, he lived in constant fear of being usurped by his children. To ensure that his children didn't revolt against him, he ended up eating his children as soon as they were born. Rhea was unhappy about the plight of her children. She decided to save at least one of their children and swapped a rock in place of the child. Cronus was tricked and this is how Zeus survived the doom that awaited him. When Zeus grew up, he instigated a rebellion against the Titan gods and led the Olympian gods into war. Once the Olympian gods succeeded, he banished the Titans to spend the rest of their lives in the underworld.

Certain myths indicate that Cronus managed to escape from the shackles of the underworld and went on to live in what is known as Italy today. He went on to rule the Italians in the name of Saturn. Stories indicate that the rule of Saturn in Italy is considered as the golden age on earth.

Dione

Dione was the daughter of the Titans, Oceanus and Tethys. It is said that she was the first wife of Zeus. Their daughter was Aphrodite. Dione was an oracular god. It is said that she shared the Oracle in Dodona with her husband and people worshipped her there. It is also said that she was the one who healed Aphrodite when she was wounded.

Eos

Eos was the daughter of Theia and Hyperion. She was regarded as the goddess of the dawn. Helios, the god of the sun, and Selene, the goddess of the moon, were her siblings. She was married to Astraeus, who was the god of the dusk. Since their union represents twilight (union of dusk and dawn), their children represent the elements of the sky, which appear at twilight. Some of their children were the five Astra Planeta (also known as wandering stars or planets) and the four Anemoi (winds).

Epimetheus

His parents were Clymene and Iapetus. His brothers were Atlas, Prometheus and Menoetius. The meaning of his name is 'afterthought' and he was regarded as a foolish character.

It was the responsibility of Prometheus and Epimetheus to award animals their different traits. It is said that he had given all the positive traits to animals and had nothing left to gift the human beings.

Certain stories indicate that the gods had gifted Pandora to Epimetheus. The daughter of Pandora and Epimetheus was Pyrrha. It was said that Pandora owned a jar, which contained all the evils relating to humanity. Pyrrha, who was curious about the contents of the jar, opened it. This resulted in all the evils entering the human world. By the time the jar was closed, it was too late. It is said that only hope remained in the jar and all the other evils had escaped.

Eurybia

Eurybia was the daughter of Gaea and Pontus. She was regarded as the goddess of the sea. She was married to Crius, and her children were Astraeus, Perses, and Pallas.

Eurynome

Eurynome was the daughter of the Titans, Oceanus and Tethys. It is said that she was the third wife of Zeus. Their union resulted in the birth of the three Charities, who were also known as the goddesses of grace.

Hyperion

Hyperion was the son of Uranus and Gaea. He was regarded as the symbol of light, watchfulness, and wisdom. He was also the father of the sun (Helios), the moon (Selene), and the dawn (Eos). He married his sister, Theia. As mentioned previously, he was one of the four pillars that were responsible for holding the earth and the heavens apart. He represented the pillar in the East. There is no conclusive proof about his participation in the war between the Olympians and the Titans. Hence, it is believed that Zeus never condemned him to spend the rest of his life in the underworld.

Iapetus

Iapetus was the son of Uranus and Gaea. He represented the pillar in the West. He was also the father of Prometheus, Atlas, Menoetius, and Epimetheus. Certain myths indicate that he was the God of mortality while other myths state that he was the god of craftsmanship.

Lelantos

Lelantos was the son of Phoebe and Coeus. It is said that he represented the element of air. Certain myths also indicate that he symbolized the hunter's skill of stalking the prey, and the unseen. Leto and Asteria were his sisters. He was married to Periboa and their union resulted in the birth of their daughter, Aura.

Menoetius

Menoetius was the son of Clymene and Iapetus. His brothers were Atlas, Epimetheus, and Prometheus. It is said that he was the god of rash actions, mortality, and violent rage. He sided with the Titans in the war against the Olympian gods. However, he was killed by Zeus and was condemned to the Tartarus in the underworld.

Metis

Metis was the daughter of the Titans, Oceanus and Tethys. It is said that she was one of the wives of Zeus. She was regarded as the goddess of wisdom, deep thought and prudence.

According to a prophecy, it was said that she would be the mother of two children, a son and a daughter. It was prophesized that the son would become more powerful than his father and overthrow him from his rule. Terrified by this prophecy, Zeus tricked Metis into transforming herself into a fly. As soon as she turned into a fly, she was swallowed by Zeus. It is said that she was pregnant with Athena when she was swallowed by Zeus. While residing inside Zeus, Metis began preparing a helmet for Athena. As Athena began growing, Zeus started experiencing an unexplainable pain on his forehead. It was so intolerable that Zeus asked Hephaestus to split open his head with an axe. When his head was opened, it is said that Athena sprang to life and was fully clothed in armor.

Mnemosyne

Mnemosyne was the daughter of Gaea and Uranus. She was regarded as the goddess of memory. Certain myths indicate that Zeus slept with her for 9 consecutive days. Their union resulted in the birth of the nine muses. It is said that Mnemosyne and her 9 muses were responsible for serving as sources of inspiration for poets and Kings across the world. They were also responsible for instilling the skill of extraordinary speech in several poets and Kings.

Oceanus

There are a couple of myths surrounding the birth of Oceanus. One myth suggests that he was the son of Chaos and Gaea. Another myth suggests that he was the son of Gaea and Uranus.

He married his sister Tethys, and their children were known as the Oceanids. The Oceanids were the goddesses of the sea, springs, and rivers. It is said that Oceanus and Tethys were so fertile that they divorced in fear of overpopulating the world with too many elements of water, which could result in floods. It is also said that Tethys and Oceanus never took part in the war between the Titans and Olympians. As a result, Zeus spared them and allowed them to continue their rule in the water.

Ophion

It was said that Ophion ruled the earth along with his wife, Eurynome. However, their positions were usurped by Rhea and Cronus, who went on to rule the earth.

Pallas

Pallas was the son of Eurybia and Crius. Astraeus and Perses were his brothers. His wife was Styx. He was regarded as the Titan god of war craft. Zelus, Nike, Scylla, Kratus, Fontes, Bia, and Lacus were his children. It is said that when the war between the Titans and the Olympians erupted, he was killed by Athena.

Phoebe

Phoebe was the daughter of Gaea and Uranus. She was married to Coeus, who was her brother. She had two daughters, Leto and

Asteria. Leto's children were Apollo and Artemis. They were also named Phoebus and Phoebe, after their grandmother.

Myths suggest that she was linked with the Oracle of Delphi and the moon. It is said that she was the goddess of prophecy. When the war erupted between the Titans and the Olympians, she took no part in the war. As a result, once the war was over, Zeus spared her and did not condemn her to spend the rest of her life in the underworld.

Prometheus

Prometheus was the son of Iapetus and Clymene. Atlas, Menoetius, and Epimetheus were his brothers. The meaning of his name is 'forethought'.

It is said that Prometheus took the side of the Olympians when the war erupted between them and the Titans. He fought alongside Zeus. As a result, he wasn't condemned to the underworld along with the other Titan gods once the war was over.

Prometheus was considered the protector of mankind. There is a famous myth about Prometheus tricking Zeus during an event called the Trick at Mecone. Zeus was asked to pick one of the two offerings for the gods. One offering involved bones tucked under glistening fat (a beautiful exterior with an inedible offering). The other offering involved the stomach of an ox, with beef studded inside (an edible offering present inside an ugly exterior). Without knowing the details of the offerings, Zeus reached out for the offering containing the glistening fat. This determined what human beings would offer to the gods to seek their blessings. Accordingly, humans consumed the meat portion and offered the bones to the gods as a sacrifice.

Zeus was enraged by this act of humans and denied them fire. Since Prometheus was the protector of mankind, he sneakily stole fire and gave it back to mankind. When Zeus came to know about this act of Prometheus, he was seething with rage. Prometheus was chained to a rock, where his liver would be eaten by eagles every day. However, the liver would regenerate every night, since Prometheus was an immortal.

Zeus was also enraged at mankind and wanted to punish them. Based on his order, Hephaestus created Pandora, who was destined to bring about all the evils into the world of humans.

Rhea

Rhea was the daughter of Uranus and Gaea. She was married to her brother, Cronus.

As already mentioned, Cronus was terrified of his children usurping his throne and thus ended up eating all of them. Rhea ended up saving Zeus by tricking Cronus. When Zeus grew up, he not only rose in rebellion against his father, but also managed to save his siblings, Poseidon, Hestia, Demeter, Hades, and Hera.

Certain myths indicate that Zeus was hidden by Rhea in a temple in Crete. She had hidden him there to save him from Cronus. Years later, people visited this temple to worship Rhea. She is depicted as a pair of lions, pulling a celestial chariot.

Selene

Selene was the daughter of Theia and Hyperion. She was regarded as the goddess of the moon. Her siblings were Helios and Eos. Selene, Hecate, and Artemis were collectively known as the lunar goddesses. It is said that Selene drove a silver moon chariot, which was being drawn by a couple of white horses. This should not be confused with the sun chariot, which is driven by four horses.

Styx

Styx was the daughter of the Titans, Oceanus and Tethys. She was regarded as the goddess of the river Styx. Her husband was Pallas. Her children were Kratos, Bia, Nike, and Zelus. It is said that during the war between the Titans and the Olympians, she sided with the Olympians and fought alongside Zeus. Once the war was over, Zeus rewarded her for her loyalty.

Tethys

Tethys was the daughter of Gaea and Uranus. It is said that she married her brother, Oceanus.

Their children were referred to as the Oceanids. Tethys raised Hera, who was brought to her by Rhea. As mentioned previously, she and her husband never took part in the war between the Titans and the Olympians. As a result, they both were spared by Zeus and were permitted to continue their reign in the sea.

Thea

Thea was the daughter of Uranus and Gaea. She was extremely beautiful and was regarded as the goddess of light. She was responsible for making silver, gold, and other precious metals and gems shine with radiance. She married her brother, Hyperion. Their union resulted in the birth of Helios, Eos, and Selene. She was also worshipped as an oracular goddess.

Themis

Themis was the daughter of Gaea and Uranus. She represented natural and moral order. She was the second wife of Zeus. It is said that Zeus' marriage to her helped him to stabilize the world and restore order.

Themis was charged with the responsibility of framing the divine laws, which governed the various gods and goddesses. It is said that she was entrusted with playing three roles. Her first role was the goddess of natural order. It is said that she performed her duties, as the goddess of natural order with the help of Hores, which made sure that time was eternal and could not be stopped. She performed her role as the goddess of natural justice through Deke (trial), Eunomia (fair order), Moires (destiny), and Erene (peace). Her third role involved her being the goddess of prophecy. She performed these duties with the help of Astraea and Nymphs. Myths indicate that she was worshipped in the Oracle of Delphi till Apollo was born.

Chapter 5: Heroes

Just as how the different deities and gods played an important role in the Greek pantheon, the heroes also played a significant part. This chapter includes a list of the important Greek heroes.

Atlanta

The parents of Atlanta are not known. However, certain myths indicate that she was abandoned by her father in a forest, right after she was born. It is said that she was raised by a bear and that she went on to become one of the finest hunters. She was famous for her skills as an exceptional archer. She was also regarded as the fastest mortal to live on earth.

Bellerophon

Bellerophon was the son of Poseidon and Eurynome. He was famous for capturing and taming the infamous Pegasus. He took part in several daring tasks, thanks to his courage, exceptional archery skills, and the assistance of Pegasus. In one of his adventures, he ended up slaying Chimaera.

His wife was Philonoe and his children were Isander, Laodameia, Hippolochus and Deidameia. Despite his many daring encounters and achievements, it was not a happy ending for Bellerophon. It was his arrogance that brought about his downfall. He aspired to reach Mount Olympus by riding Pegasus. However, Zeus stopped him midway, which resulted in him falling down the mountain. This fall crippled him forever.

Heracles (Hercules)

Several myths state that Heracles was the strongest mortal on earth. When the Olympians went into war against the Giants, Heracles had sided with the Olympians and helped them win the war. There is another myth that suggests that Heracles was the last mortal son of Zeus. Physical strength was the only thing that came to Heracles' aid, for he was neither wise nor intelligent. Whenever things did not coax his pride, he took offense instantly. He was infamous for holding personal grudges. He was not one to easily forget. It is also said that he possessed a bad temper and was known for his reckless nature.

Meleager

Meleager was the son of King Oeneus and Althaea. He was famous for his bravery as well as nobility. His wife was Cleopatra, and Polydora was his daughter. However, his peaceful life was shattered when Artemis unleashed a wild boar, which threatened the lives of the people in his Kingdom. During his attempt to hunt the boar, he was killed by it.

Perseus

Perseus was the son of Danae and Zeus. His mother was the daughter of King Acrisius. It is said that he was the first hero to have lived in the Greek pantheon. Apollo had foretold that Perseus would be responsible for bringing about the death of his grandfather. Fearing his death, King Acrisius had banished both his daughter and Perseus from his kingdom.

Perseus grew up into a brave, young man. There are several myths, which talk about his courage and bravery. When several brave men failed in killing Medusa, he succeeded. He also saved Andromeda, who was left to die in the hands of Cetua, the sea monster. It was Poseidon who had condemned her to such a fate. However, things took a turn for good, when Perseus saved her. They ended up marrying and lived together happily for several years.

As per the prophecy, he did eventually kill his grandfather. He met his end in the hands of Dionysus.

Theseus

Theseus was a hero, who was celebrated for not just his intelligence and wisdom but also for his bravery and strength. Several tales talk about the shrewdness exhibited by him in politics. He was loved by the Athenians for his several contributions towards the growth of the city.

With the passage of time, his wisdom faded and he created a lot of chaos and confusion. He started losing respect in the eyes of fellow Athenians and was ultimately exiled. It is said that he died alone, while in exile.

Chapter 6: Monsters and Creatures

The Greek pantheon was marked by exciting and interesting magical creatures. At the same time, it was also filled with monsters. These creatures and monsters proved to be a source of inspiration for many poets and writers!

Argus Panoptes

Argus Panoptes was a giant, who had hundreds of eyes. He was also known as Argos. His father was Arestor. He served the goddess Hera. His primary responsibility was to guard Io, the nymph, with whom Zeus was having an affair. With Argos standing guard, it was not possible for Zeus to visit Io undetected. He solicited the help of Hermes, who disguised himself as a shepherd and put Argos to sleep. Once he drifted off to sleep, he was killed by Hermes.

Ash Tree nymphs

The Ash tree nymphs were born from the blood drops that got spilt on the earth, when Uranus was castrated by Cronus. The nymphs are also collectively known as Meliae. It is also said that the giants and Erinyes were born out of Uranus' blood drops. Certain myths also suggest that the human beings belonging to the Bronze Age originated from the ash tree nymphs.

Centaurs

Centaurs were half human and half horse creatures. They had the torso, head, and arms of a man, while their lower body was that of a horse. Centaurs were regarded as lustful creatures and known for their wildness.

The only centaur who was an exception, was Chiron. Chiron was extremely modest and was known for his teaching abilities. He was also known for his knowledge in medicine. He was an immortal and served as the tutor for several gods.

Cerberus

Cerberus was entrusted with the responsibility of guarding the entrance of the underworld. Myths suggest that he was a dog with three heads. It is also said that he had a mane of snakes, a serpent as a tail, and the claws of a lion. It was his responsibility to allow the dead souls enter the underworld. He also ensured that nobody left the underworld. He is believed to be the son of Typhon and Echidna.

Chimaera

Chimaera was also the child of Typhon and Echidna. It is said that Chimaera had the head and body of a lion. The tail ended with the head of a snake. A goat's head was attached on the back of Chimaera's head. By breathing fire, Chimaera was responsible for torching many lands. Chimaera was killed by Bellerophon, who achieved this task with the help of Pegasus.

Chrysaor

Chrysaor was the son of Medusa and Poseidon. Pegasus was his brother. It is believed that Pegasus and Chrysaor came into existence when Medusa was beheaded by Perseus. Chrysaor was known as a warrior with a tough heart.

Cyclopes

The Cyclopes were monsters, which had only one eye. There are several myths surrounding the birth of the Cyclopes. Certain myths suggest that they were born from the union of Uranus and Gaea. Other myths indicate that they were the children of Poseidon. They grew at the same rate as giants. The eye was situated in the center of the forehead. These Cyclopes did not fear gods and did not follow any laws.

It was said that the Cyclopes were represented by Polyphemus. However, he was outwitted and blinded by Odysseus.

Literature draws reference to three important Cyclopes, namely; Arges (thunderbolt), Steropes (lightning), and Brontes (thunder). When Cronus came into power, after overthrowing his father, the first thing he did was to banish all the Cyclopes to the underworld. They were freed by Zeus when the war between the Titans and Olympians began. As a token of gratitude, they gifted the lightning and thunderbolt to Zeus, which later became his weapons.

Echidna

Echidna was regarded as the mother of all monsters. She was half maiden and half snake. She was married to the monster, Typhon. He was regarded as the father of all monsters. Typhon and Echidna were born from the union of Tartarus and Gaea. When Typhon and Echidna were engaged in a revolt against the Olympians, they were defeated by Zeus, and Typhon was buried under Mount Etna. Zeus, however, spared the lives of Echidna and her children.

Some of the notable children of Typhon and Echidna include Cerberus, Chimaera, the Gorgon sisters, and the Lernaean Hydra, the creature with several heads.

Giants

As already mentioned, they originated from the blood drops of Uranus. They were regarded as a race of immense strength. The war between the Olympians and the giants is regarded as one of the important events in Greek mythology. The Olympians won the war and ended up ruling the giants. A few notable giants were Eurymedon, Porphyrion, and Enceladus.

Gorgons

Gorgons were the daughters of Typhon and Echidna, and they were Euryale, Medusa, and Stheno. It was said that Medusa was a mortal whereas her sisters were immortal. Certain myths state that Medusa's mortality can be attributed to her birth. These myths actually suggest that Keto and Phorkys were the parents of Medusa. All the three sisters had snakes coiled up on their heads, instead of hair. It is said that all the three sisters looked gruesome and were capable of turning anybody into stone with their gazes.

According to certain myths, Medusa was not born ugly. She was a beautiful maiden and had golden hair. She had taken the oath of celibacy and was a priestess of Athena. It is said that Poseidon was awestruck by her beauty and tried to win her over. Charmed by Poseidon, Medusa forgot her oath of celibacy and fell in love with him. She ended up marrying him. Athena was furious about her breach of oath and went on to punish Medusa. Her golden hair turned into snakes. Her lustful and beautiful eyes turned bloodshot. Anybody who looked her in the eye would be instantly filled with fear and disgust. Her fair skin turned an ugly green.

It is said that Medusa was repulsed by her own appearance and she decided to run away from home. When the entire world began to shun her, she decided to become a monster. Because of

Athena's curse, Medusa also had the power to turn anybody into stone, if they ever looked her in the eye. She went on to terrorize others until she met her end at the hands of Perseus.

Hecatoncheires

These were giants with a hundred hands and fifty heads. They were born from the union of Uranus and Gaea, and were representative of huge sea waves and earthquakes. The three Hecatoncheires were Aegaeon, Gyges, and Cottus.

Pegasus

Pegasus was a white, flying horse, who was born when Medusa was beheaded. Bellerphon captured Pegasus and ensured that he was tamed. Pegasus aided Bellerophon in his various quests, including slaying Chimaera.

Sirens

The sirens are regarded as beautiful as well as dangerous creatures in Greek mythology. It is believed that they were capable of luring in sailors, who would pass them on their voyages. It is said that their voices were capable of causing ships to crash into their island.

Certain myths suggest that the sirens were the companions of Persephone. Persephone was the daughter of the goddess, Demeter. According to these myths, the goddess had granted each siren a pair of wings, to protect her daughter. When Hades kidnapped Persephone and took her to the underworld, Demeter was filled with rage. She is believed to have cursed the sirens for not protecting her daughter. It is said that the sirens were singing a sad melody, ever since Persephone was abducted, waiting for her to return.

Chapter 7: Stories about Zeus

We have already learned about Zeus' birth, his wrath, and about his infidelities to a certain extent. There are many other stories of Zeus however, which we will discuss in this chapter.

Zeus' fight with Typhon

Once the Olympians defeated the Titans, it is believed that Gaea, Mother Earth, was extremely angry with Zeus. She believed that her sons, the Titans, were treated in an unfair and irrational manner by Zeus.

To defeat Zeus and restore the Titans back to power, Gaea conceived a plan. She united with Tartarus, which symbolized the underworld. This result in the creation of a deadly monster, named the Typhon.

Typhon was not only frightening to look at but also possessed several powers. He went on to attack the homes of the gods by throwing flaming rocks at them, burning their houses. He terrified the gods by breathing flames out of his mouth. It is said that the gods were so terrified that they ran away to Egypt and transformed themselves into animals.

While all this was happening, Zeus was silent. Athena confronted him and accused him of being a coward. Offended by Athena's remarks, Zeus decided to take on the monster. With his thunderbolt in one hand and the sickle in the other, he struck the monster. He kept chasing the monster till they reached Mount Casion, which is located in what we know as Syria today.

Typhon became gravely injured in the process, at which point Zeus decided to engage the monster in a hand to hand fight.

When Zeus was least expecting it, Typhon wrapped Zeus in his coils and squeezed him. While holding on to Zeus firmly, he tried to pry away the sickle from Zeus' hand. Once he was successful in wrestling the sickle from Zeus, he cut the tendons from Zeus' feet and hands. He then dragged Zeus to the Corycian cave. The cave was situated on the slopes of Mount Parnassus. Here, he entrusted his sister, Delphyne, who was half dragon and half maiden, with the responsibility of guarding Zeus.

We already know how Hermes was quick and light footed. He managed to sneak in along with Aigipan, and was successful in fitting Zeus' tendons back together. As soon as Zeus regained some of his strength, he made a steep descent from the heavens. He went on to chase Typhon aggressively, while directing his thunderbolts at the monster. When they reached the island of Sicily, it is said that Zeus brought the monster down by throwing Mount Etna at him. Typhon was pinned desperately under the enormous mountain.

It is believed that the volcanic eruptions from Mount Etna are caused by the thunderbolts of Zeus.

Zeus and the island of Aegina

It is said that Zeus fell in love with Aegina. She was one of the 20 daughters of Asopus, who was the god of rivers. She was the most beautiful among her sisters. Captivated by her beauty, Zeus kidnapped her and took her to a small island, Oenone. Their union resulted in the birth of their son, Aeacus. Aeacus went on to become the King of the island and named the island after his mother.

To ensure that the island was well populated and strong, Zeus transformed all the ants present on the island into warriors. These warriors wore black armor and had 6 hands. Since ants were referred to as myrmigia in Greek, the island was also known as Myrmidons.

It is said that Achilles, a Greek hero, later commanded the inhabitants of this island, who were known as the fiercest Greek warriors.

Zeus and the bees

One fine day, the bee, also known as the mother of candles, decided to visit the gods. While paying her respects, the bee offered the gods honey and honeycombs. Zeus, who was pleased with the bee's gifts decided to grant her a wish. When he asked her what she wanted, she asked Zeus to give her a sting, which will help her protect the fruit of her labors (the honey). Since Zeus was also the protector of human beings, he granted the bee's wish with a condition. The bee's sting will most certainly help her protect her honey from humans who try to steal it. However, if she decides to sting humans for no reason, she would immediately die.

Zeus and the greedy ant

It is said that when the world was first created, there were no ants. Zeus found out that man was extremely greedy and was trying to scrounge the labors of other men. To teach humans a lesson, Zeus converted greedy men into ants. This is how ants came into existence. However, it is said that this attempt never changed the habits of men. Humans still exhibit the trait of greed and try scrounging the fruits of others' labors.

Zeus and the tortoise

When Zeus decided to get married, he wanted to invite all the animals to his wedding. While all the animals were present at the wedding, the tortoise was absent. Zeus noticed this absence and was puzzled by it. He could not understand why the tortoise would miss such a feast! He went and asked the tortoise the reason behind its absence from the grand celebrations. The tortoise replied that there was no place better than its house! Offended by the tortoise's reply, Zeus forced it to forever carry its home on its back.

Chapter 8: Heracles and his 12 labors

In this section, we shall go through the twelve tasks of Heracles (Hercules). As the legend goes, Heracles was filled with remorse after killing his wife and children. He sought guidance from Apollo on the nature of the penance he should do for his wrongdoings. Apollo instructed Heracles to go to King Eurystheus and serve him for twelve years. Eurystheus, in turn, sent Heracles to perform 12 seemingly impossible tasks. The following are the twelve tasks that Heracles performed for King Eurystheus.

1. Slaying the Nemean Lion

The Nemean lion tormented the region of Nemea by taking young pretty women from the surrounding villages as hostages. The abducted women were taken to its cave in the mountains. Warriors from the villages who came to the cave to rescue the damsels in distress would fall prey to the Nemean lion, which would then proceed to devour them.

Heracles, once entrusted with the task of slaying the lion, went up to the lair of the beast. He had prepared for the hunt by gathering arrows. But when he shot the arrows at the lion, they simply bounced off its fur, which was apparently impenetrable armor. He then had to resort to brute force by clubbing the beast after closing off one of the entrances of its lair to prevent escape. He strangled the stunned beast and skinned it to use the hide and fur as his personal armor.

2. Slaying the Lernaean Hydra

The next task was to slay the monstrous Lernaean Hydra. When Heracles reached the lake Lerna, he braved through the poisonous fumes emitted by the Hydra and started firing blazing arrows at it. Some stories claim that he used a sickle while some others say it was a sword, to cut the heads off the Hydra. But he found that, for every head he cut off, two others grew back.

In despair, he turned to his nephew Iolaus for assistance. Iolaus came up with the plan of burning off each neck stump after Heracles cut off the head. The Hydra had one immortal head and Heracles used a golden sword to cut it off, thus slaying the beast. He then dipped his arrows in the poisonous blood of the Hydra.

3. Capturing the Ceryneian Hind

The next task given by King Eurystheus was to capture the Ceryneian Hind. The hind was so fast that it could outrun a shot arrow, hence making its capture a seemingly impossible task. Heracles pursued the animal for a year all through Greece, Istria, and Thrace. There are many versions of this story. Some state that he caught the hind with a net while it was asleep, while some others claim that Heracles shot an arrow through its forelegs, thereby trapping it.

The hind was the sacred animal of the temple of Artemis, and to avoid her wrath, Heracles had to promise the goddess that he would free the hind after displaying it to Eurystheus and that capturing the hind was part of his penance.

4. Capturing the Erymanthian Boar

The Erymanthian Boar was a giant, fearsome animal that lived on Mount Erymanthos. King Eurystheus asked Heracles to capture the boar, confident that the difficulty of the task would ensure failure of Heracles. On his way to capture the boar, Heracles met his friend Pholus, a centaur. He then proceeded to dine with Pholus and his other companion centaurs. The other centaurs attacked Heracles in a drunken trance and he had to fend them off with his poisonous arrows. A stray arrow also hit Chiron, a friendly immortal centaur.

In pain, Chiron exchanged his immortality, only to be chained to the mountain, instead of Prometheus, and had to endure his liver being eaten by the eagle. Heracles helped his friend by killing the eagle and in return, Chiron told him how to capture the boar by running it into thick snow in the winter. Heracles was thus able to complete the task.

5. Cleaning the Augean Stables

Heracles was next given the humiliating and extremely difficult task of cleaning the stables of King Augeas. The task was considered impossible because the enormous stable contained 1,000 animals and had not been cleaned in 30 years. Before he began the task, Heracles struck a deal with Augeas to receive payment in the form of one-tenth of the cattle if the stables were cleaned in a day.

Heracles performed the task by diverting the two rivers – Alpheus and Peneus through the stables. However, King Eurystheus declined to accept the task because Heracles had made the rivers do the cleaning and also because he took payment for doing so.

6. Slaying the Stymphalian Birds

Heracles' next task was to kill the Stymphalian birds. These birds were fearsome man-eaters and were sacred to the god

Ares. These birds were many in number, and to make matters worse, they had metallic feathers for weapons and strong beaks made of bronze.

Heracles was however successful in killing most of the birds with his poisonous arrows. A few of them did escape his slaughter but this task was considered as completed.

7. Capturing the Cretan Bull

The enormous bull lived in Crete where it tormented the countryside by destroying crops and leveling houses. Heracles sailed to Crete and was offered assistance by King Minos in capturing the bull. Heracles declined the help and embarked to capture the gigantic animal. Heracles wrestled with the bull for hours before strangling it and forcing it to the ground.

He then brought the captured bull to Eurystheus, who was so frightened by the monstrous animal that he immediately ordered it to be released.

8. Capturing the Mares of Diomedes

The mares of Diomedes had a frightening reputation for being mad horses that breathed fire and consumed human flesh. They had been reared this way by the King Diomedes. The animals were indeed difficult to capture but Heracles somehow managed to capture them. However, now he had to fight off Diomedes and his army who had pursued him.

Heracles left the horses in the care of Abderus, his companion, and went to fight Diomedes. Upon returning, he found that Abderus had been eaten by the uncontrollable mares. This enraged Heracles, and in revenge he killed Diomedes and fed him to the mares to calm them. He then took them to King Eurystheus.

9. Retrieving the Belt of Hippolyta

Heracles's ninth task was to retrieve the belt of Hippolyta, the queen of the Amazons. He was to fetch the belt for Admete, daughter of Eurystheus. Heracles set sail for Themiscyra, where Hippolyta lived with the rest of the Amazons. Hippolyta had heard of the brave and strong Heracles and was impressed with his feats. She would have gladly parted her belt had he asked for it.

However, Hera decided to deceive Heracles and spread lies in Themiscyra that Heracles was coming to abduct their queen Hippolyta. The enraged Amazons decided to fight Heracles. He killed them and their Queen, and took her belt.

10.   Capturing the Cattle of Geryon

The tenth task for Heracles was to capture the cattle of Geryon in Erytheia. When Heracles reached Erytheia, he was attacked by the two-headed guard dog, Orthrus. Heracles killed Orthrus using his club. He then had to face Geryon himself, who had come prepared to fight Heracles. He was killed using one of the poisoned arrows that Heracles had dipped in the Hydra's blood.

Heracles then proceeded to herd the cattle back to Eurystheus. He had to face many other difficulties on the way back, which were thrown at him by Hera, but Heracles triumphed over them all and successfully delivered the cattle to Eurystheus.

11.   Stealing the Apples of Hesperides

After Eurysytheus discounted two of the labors, Heracles was given two additional ones. His eleventh task was to steal the apples from the garden of Hesperides. There are two versions of the story as to how Heracles managed to procure the apples. In the first version, after reaching the garden of Hesperides, he meets Atlas who was holding the heavens up on his shoulders. Heracles asked Atlas to fetch him apples and in return, offered to hold the heavens aloft while Atlas was gone. When Atlas came back, he planned to trick Heracles by not taking the heavens back and instead offered to deliver the apples himself. Heracles was smarter and feigning acceptance, asked Atlas to hold the heavens while he adjusted his armor. He then walked away with the apples.

In another version, Heracles had to fight and slay Ladon, the dragon, who guarded the apples.

12.   Capturing Cerberus

The final task for Heracles was to capture Cerberus, the three-headed dog that guards the underworld. Heracles approached Hades, the god of the underworld for his approval. Hades agreed to Heracles's demand on the sole condition that Cerberus should not be captured using any weapons. Heracles thus fought Cerberus and finally brought him to the surface, after overpowering him with his strength.

When he took the captured Cerberus to Eurystheus, the King was so frightened at seeing the dog that he pleaded Heracles to take the creature back to the underworld and in return, offered to release Heracles from the obligation to perform any more tasks.

Chapter 9: Hyacinth

Hyacinth was a mortal, who was known for his beauty. There are several myths surrounding the parentage of Hyacinth. Certain myths indicate that he was the son of Pierus and Clios, while others state that he was the son of King Oebalus of Sparta. Another myth suggests that he was the son of King Amyclas of Sparta.

It is said that Hyacinth was a handsome youth, and that he was also the lover of Apollo. He also found an admirer in Zephyrus, the west wind. One day, Apollo and Hyacinth were engaged in a game of discus. They both took turns in throwing the discus. When Apollo threw the discus, Hyacinth ran to catch it, with a view to impress Apollo. Unfortunately, he was struck by the discus and was killed by it.

There is another myth surrounding the death of Hyacinth. Apparently, it was Zephyrus jealousy that brought about Hyacinth's death. According to this myth, Zephyrus was extremely jealous of the relationship shared by Apollo and Hyacinth. When he saw Hyacinth chasing the discus thrown by Apollo, Zephyrus blew the discus in the direction of Hyacinth, which struck him and killed him.

Heartbroken by Hyacinth's death, Apollo did not let Hades claim the soul of Hyacinth. Instead, he converted him into a flower to continue existing. This is how the flower hyacinth came into existence. Another myth suggests that Apollo's tears of grief stained the petals of the flower forever.

Spartans celebrate the death of Hyacinth at Amyclae in the Spartan month of Hyacinthius. The festival lasts for three days in the summer. The first day starts with grieving for the death of

Hyacinth. The last two days involves people celebrating the rebirth of Hyacinth as a flower, and the glory of Apollo.

Chapter 10: Pandora's Box

Pandora was the first woman on earth, according to myth. She was created under the order of Zeus, and was formed from clay, sculpted by Hermes.

After Prometheus disobeyed Zeus' orders and gave humans fire, Pandora was created as a punishment to humankind. Upon her creation, Pandora was given gifts from each of the Gods, from beauty, to curiosity, to musical ability. These gifts formed her personality, and created a cunning and curious woman.

Pandora was also given a box, with unknown things inside; but was instructed to never open the box. The box was filled with different evil things, that should never be released onto the world. However, one of the personality traits she had been given was curiosity, making it difficult for her to restrain from opening the box.

Hermes took Pandora to Epimetheus, the brother of Prometheus in order to have them wed. Prometheus was not in good favor with the Gods, and had advised his brother to not accept any gifts from them. Pandora's beauty however was too great, and Epimetheus accepted her as his wife right away.

Pandora struggled for a time to refrain from opening the box, but eventually her curiosity prevailed. When she opened the box, all of the horrors known to humankind escaped. Strife, sickness, toil, and a range of other terrors escaped the box and were released unto the world.

Before all of the contents escaped, Pandora was able to close the box with just one thing left inside of it – hope.

The phrase 'Pandora's box' stems from this story, and is often used to describe a taking a seemingly small and innocent action that then creates a lot of problems! When we don't know how dire the consequences will be of a small action, it is as if we opened up Pandora's box.

The above was the most common version of the story, but there are several different variations of this tale. In many, the 'box' is actually referred to as a jar. The changing of the story to a 'box' only occurred in the 16th century, when it was translated to Latin. Since then, the phrase 'Pandora's box' has grown famous.

In some versions of the story, the box was actually in the possession of Epimetheus prior to their marriage, and Pandora simply found it in his home.

Chapter 11: Trojan War

The Trojan war was a battle between the people of Greece, and the people of the city of Troy.

King Priam was the ruler of the wealthy city of Troy. He had many children, and the future seemed very bright for the King and his family. However, one night his wife, Hecuba, had a nightmare in which she gave birth to a deadly firebrand. The seers interpreted this to mean that her unborn child would destroy Troy and its inhabitants. When the child was born, he was disposed of at Mount Ida. King Priam thought that the child had surely died alone at the mountain, but actually he survived, and was raised by a she-bear. The child grew up to be a shepherd, named Paris.

At the wedding of Peleus and Thetis, the gods were enjoying themselves when Eris threw a golden apple into their midst with the words, "For the fairest". Hera, Athena, and Aphrodite all tried to claim the apple as their own. An argument erupted over who was the most deserving. After coming to no conclusion, they asked Zeus to judge between them and choose the fairest. Zeus refused to choose, and instead directed the three goddesses to a shepherd on Mount Ida who could decide who he thought was the most deserving. The shepherd was of course, none other than Paris.

The goddesses approached Paris and each tried to bribe him to select her as the fairest. Hera promised to make him a king who would rule Asia and have great wealth. Athena offered to give him wisdom and invincibility in warfare. Aphrodite was the winner however, as she offered Paris the most beautiful woman in the world - the stunning Helen. This of course made Paris a happy man, but in doing so Paris made powerful enemies of both Hera and Athena. They both vowed to destroy Paris, and also the city of Troy.

Excited to soon be with Helen, Paris returned to Troy, where he exposed himself as a true prince, and the legitimate son of Priam and Hecuba. With no further use for his previous love Oenone, he left her. He the proceeded to sail to Sparta. While there, he seduced Helen during her husband's absence, before returning to Troy with her.

At the same time, Paris' sister Cassandra was in trouble. Apollo gave her the gift of prophecy in an attempt to make love to her, but she had taken a vow of chastity and so, resisted him. In retribution, Apollo transformed his gift into a curse by making it so that no one would believe her prophecies. When Paris returned with Helen and stood before Priam to ask his father's acceptance, Cassandra burst into the room. She prophesized that incredible suffering would be caused by the actions of her lusting brother. Of course, due to the curse, nobody believed this prophecy. Priam thought that Cassandra was mad, and had his own daughter locked in a cell.

When Menelaus returned to Sparta and found that his wife Helen had abandoned him for Paris, he summoned the Greek leaders, and together they set off to to conquer Troy and recover Helen. Thus began the Trojan war. The prophetic dream his mother had of giving birth to a firebrand that would eventually lead to the destruction of Troy had come to life.

The Greek chieftains assembled at Aulis under the leadership of Agamemnon, the brother of Menelaus. The majority of the warriors were enthusiastic about the journey, and were eager to conquer Troy. However, not all in Greece wanted to join the cause.

Odysseus was told by an oracle that he would be away from home for 20 years if he went on the journey, and so he pretended to be overcome with madness when the Greek leaders came to recruit him. Palamedes exposed the act, and Odysseus was forced to go. It would have been impossible for the Greeks to take Troy without the help of Achilles, and so the Greeks went to Scyros to recruit him. Achilles was almost completely invulnerable as a fighter, because his mother, Thetis, had dipped him in the River Styx at birth, rendering him immortal everywhere but in his heel. Achilles was famous for his abilities as an incredible warrior. He knew that he would have a short but glorious life if he went to Troy, and so he had his mother disguise him in women's clothing at the Scyrian court. However, Odysseus discovered Achilles, and he too eventually consented to go.

At first the Greeks sailed to Mysia, believing that it was Troy. Because of this mistake, they started war with the Mysians. The Mysian king, Telephus, was wounded in the battle by Achilles.

 Learning of their geographical mistake, the Greeks sailed back to Aulis. Since an oracle had said that Troy could not be taken without the advice of Telephus', Achilles was obliged to heal him. The Trojan prophet, Calchas, had sided with the Greeks, and when unfavorable winds prevented the Greeks from sailing, Calchas declared that the goddess Artemis wanted the sacrifice of a virgin. Agamemnon's daughter Iphigenia was chosen and sent for under the pretext that she would marry Achilles.

According to most versions of the tale, upon discovering the real reason she had been summoned, Iphigenia willingly allowed herself to be sacrificed for the Greek cause. After the sacrifice was made, the weather improved, and the Greeks continued onwards to Troy.

An oracle had prophesized that the first man to step foot onshore Trojan territory would be the first to lose their life. Protesilaus took this burden on himself, and was engaged in a losing skirmish with Hector, the Trojan prince.

Hector, a great warrior, bore the knowledge that both he and his city were doomed. They simply did not have enough great warriors to win the war. Troy did have one defender worth noting however, Aeneas, an ally from a neighboring land. The Greek army, however, was full of heroes. There was Agamemnon, Menelaus, Nestor, Odysseus, and Achilles, along with Diomedes and the two Ajaxes.

The gods intervened in the war occasionally also, sometimes deciding the outcome of various battles. Apollo, Artemis, Ares, and Aphrodite sided with the Trojans, while Hera, Athena, Poseidon, Hermes, and Hephaestus aided the Greeks. Zeus only interfered on occasion. For the most part though he maintained a neutral stance.

After nine years of fighting, the Greeks had destroyed many kingdoms that were allies of Troy in Asia, but they had not made much progress against Troy itself. There was a lot of tension between the Greeks. Odysseus still held a grudge against Palamedes, the man who had ruthlessly shown his madness to be a hoax, forcing him to join the war. When Palamedes denounced Odysseus for taking them on an unsuccessful foraging expedition, Odysseus framed Palamedes, making him appear to be a traitor. Palamedes was sentenced to death by stoning as a result.

Later in the war however, an even more problematic argument occurred. This time it was between Agamemnon and Achilles. Agamemnon had taken the daughter of a priest as a trophy of war, and when her father came to ransom her, Agamemnon sent him away without her. The priest called upon Apollo to assist him, and so Apollo sent a plague to the Greeks that killed many. Achilles called upon the council and demanded that Agamemnon give back the girl, Chryseis, to her father. Agamemnon reluctantly agreed, but insisted on taking Achilles' own prize, the maid Briseis, as a replacement. This suggestion would have resulted in murder had Athena not intervened. Achilles reluctanctly gave up Briseis, and also decided to withdraw from the war. Since the Greek victories up to that point had been a result of Achilles' strength and ability in battle, this was a huge problem for the Greeks. Achilles told his mother, Thetis, to petition Zeus for Trojan victories, which she did.

Once they saw that Achilles and his closest comrades had withdrawn from the war, the Trojans made an attack. Agamemnon decided to grant a truce in which it was agreed that Paris and Menelaus would fight in single combat for Helen. But the duel was inconclusive, for Aphrodite, seeing that Paris was losing, wrapped him in a magic cloud and took him back to Troy.

Menelaus searched for Paris in the Trojan ranks, and Agamemnon demanded that the Trojans surrender Helen. The

Trojans were willing to concede, and end the war without any more death or destruction. However, Hera had different ideas, and desperately wanted Troy destroyed. Hera sent Athena to break the truce, and to continue the war. Athena persuaded the Trojan archer Pandarus to fire an arrow at Menelaus. The shot grazed Menelaus, and the fighting resumed once again.

The great Ajax and Diomedes fought in a forceful manner, killing dozens and dozens of Trojans. Diomedes killed Pandarus and wounded Aeneas. Aphrodite came to rescue her son Aeneas, but Diomedes managed to wound her wrist, causing the goddess to flee. However, Apollo retrieved Aeneas from the field and he was then cured by Artemis. Diomedes then encountered Hector, who was accompanied by the fearsome Ares, the god of battle. Diomedes was intimidated by the god, and the Greeks retreated. Athena, however gave Diomedes the courage to attack Ares. Ares was injured, and crying in pain he fled to Olympus.

Hector was forced to retreat, and was advised to return to Troy and plead to his mother Hecuba for mercy from Athena. He offered her the most beautiful robe in exchange for this deed. His mother agreed, but the plea failed to please the goddess. After a discussion with his wife Andromache, Hector returned to the battlefield and issued a challenge to duel to Achilles. He declined and instead, Ajax accepted the challenge. In the ensuing fight, Ajax slightly bested Hector. The two warriors parted afterwards, and exchanged gifts as a sign of respect.

Thetis asked Zeus to aid the Trojans, by ordering the other gods to leave the battlefield. Zeus agreed, and consequentially, the Greeks lost badly. Under Hector's relentless assault, the Greeks were almost forced into retreat by evening. Disheartened, Agamemnon considered abandoning the siege of Troy. However, Nestor, who was old and wise, recommended that he make peace with Achilles by giving him back Briseis, and a pile of wealth to boot. The great warrior Achilles listened to the proposal from Agamemnon, but respectfully refused the offer. His pride was at stake, and he would only fight if he or his Myrmidons were threatened. The situation seemed hopeless to most, but nonetheless, that night Odysseus and Diomedes raided the Trojan camp and killed many, including King Rhesus.

The next day the Greeks were forced to retreat even further to the beach where their boats were, and Agamemnon, Odysseus, and Diomedes were wounded. The war seemed all but over when Hera decided that she would turn the tide of thebattle. Using Aphrodite's magic girdle, she seduced Zeus and distracted him from the war. While Zeus was occupied, Poseidon returned to the battle and forced the Trojans into retreat. Ajax hurled a boulder at Hector which knocked him down, whereupon the Trojans stampeded madly for the city. Once Zeus had recovered from his infatuation, he saw the chaos and threatened to beat Hera. Once again, he also ordered Poseidon from the field.

Hector was aided by Apollo, bringing him back to health. With Hector at the forefront, the Trojans beat down the barricades the Greeks had put in place to protect their ships, bringing the war back in their favor. Greatly worried, Achilles' companion Patroclus tried to persuade his friend to fight, but once again Achilles refused. Instead, Patroclus borrowed Achilles' armor and entered the battle, masquerading as the great warrior. Thinking that the armored warrior was in fact Achilles, the Trojans began to panic. Patroclus fought well, and slaughtered many. He continued his onslaught until he reached the walls of Troy, where Apollo dazed him as he tried to scale them. At the city wall, Hector faced Patroclus, and defeated him in battle, stripping him of his borrowed armor.

Upon hearing the news of Patroclus' death, Achilles was distraught and overcome with grief. He wished to avenge the death of his good friend, and so his mother, Thetis, brought him new armor fashioned by Hephaestus. Upon presenting him the armor, she warned him that if he avenged his friend by killing Hector, that he himself would perish soon after. This did not deter Achilles, who was determined to kill not only Hector, but also as many Trojans as possible. The following day, he made a formal reconciliation with Agamemnon and entered the battle immediately, much to the delight of the Greeks.

The clash of arms that day was the most incredible yet. Hector and Aeneas slaughtered scores of Greeks, but they were no match for Achilles in his revenge-driven fury. During the day's battles, both Aeneas and Hector had to be rescued from Achilles through divine intervention. Achilles went on to fill the Scamander River so full of bodies that the waters over-flowed, nearly drowning him. The Gods also engaged in battle on this day. They fought amongst themselves, as Athena felled Ares, Hera boxed Artemis' ears, and Poseidon provoked Apollo.

Finally, Achilles found Hector outside the walls of Troy. Hector feared Achilles, and ran from his opponent, circling the city three times. Athena then fooled him into making a stand, and fighting Achilles. He was no match for Achilles, whose lance caught him in the throat. As Hector died, he begged Achilles to let his parents ransom his body, but Achilles denied him jeeringly. Instead, Achilles took Hector's corpse, tied it behind his chariot, and dragged it back to the Greek camp victorious, as Hector's wife watched from the walls of Troy.

Shortly after, Patroclus' ghost appeared to Achilles, and demanded a proper burial for himself. Achilles prepared a glorious funeral for Patroclus. He slit the throats of twelve Trojan nobles as a sacrifice on Patroclus' pyre. After the funeral, there were contests in athletics to honor his late friend. Over the next eleven days, Achilles celebrated his revenge by dragging Hector's body around the pyre, as Apollo preserved the corpse from corruption for him. Zeus then commanded Thetis to plead with Achilles to accept the ransom offered by King Priam for Hector's body. Zeus also sent Hermes to King Priam, instructing him to safely escort the King to Achilles' camp. Achilles treated King Priam courteously, as Priam reminded him of his own father, Peleus. Achilles agreed to the King's terms, and took Hector's weight in gold in exchange for the body. Priam took Hector's body back to the city of Troy. During the next eleven days there was an agreed upon truce and break in the fighting, as the Trojans mourned for the dead Hector, whom they cremated and buried.

Once the fighting resumed, Achilles remained on the battlefield. His next notable victory was against the Amazon Queen, Penthesileia. Despite their losses, the Trojans were not yet finished. They brought in Ethiopian reinforcements under Prince Memnon, which made things challenging for the Greeks. These reinforcements fought well, and many Greeks were killed.

When the warrior Prince Memnon killed Achilles' friend
Antilochus in battle, Achilles retaliated by killing Memnon in a
duel. However, according to his mother's prophecy, Achilles' life
was soon to end, which he well knew. One day not long after his
duel with Memnon, Paris shot at Achilles with a poison arrow.
Apollo guided the arrow, directing it to Achilles' right heel, the
only place where he was vulnerable, ending the great warrior's
life. The Greeks had a difficult time retrieving his body from the
battlefield, but eventually, Ajax and retrieved it from the
Trojans. The Greek hero was given a magnificent funeral.

Shortly after the funeral, an argument arose as to whether Ajax
or Odysseus should receive Achilles' powerful armor. The Greek
commanders voted on it, with Odysseus being declared the
winner. This infuriated Ajax, who believed he was more worthy
of the armor. In retaliation, Ajax resolved to kill a number of the
Greek leaders, including Odysseus himself. But during the night,
Athena visited him and afflicted him with madness. In his
crazed state, Ajax butchered a number of cattle under the
delusion that they were the men who had voted against him.
Athena then removed the madness she had inflicted upon him,
and Ajax realized what he had done. He was overcome with the
shame of his actions, and proceeded to commit suicide.

Now suddenly, Greece was in a dire situation. Two of their best
heroes were dead, which left them anxious about taking Troy.
Using brute force had been unsuccessful thus far, and so the
Greeks began to turn to the use of oracles for advice. Calchas the
oracle informed them that they needed the bow and arrows of
Heracles to win the war. These items were currently in the
hands of Prince Philoctetes. The Prince was a warrior that the
Greeks had abandoned years before on the island of Lemnos.
They left him there whilst heading to Troy, due to him being
wounded and failing to heal. Odysseus and Diomedes were sent
to Lemnos to fetch the weapons. Once there, Odysseus tricked
Philoctetes into handing over the bow and arrows. Odysseus
then prepared to leave, but Diomedes kindly offered to take
Philoctetes back to Troy with them, so that he could finally be
cured of his wounds. Although he was bitter at losing his
weapons, Philoctetes agreed. Together, they sailed for Troy, and
once there, Paris was killed with the arrows of Heracles. Paris

did have a chance to survive, but his former mistress, the nymph Oenone, refused to heal him out of spite.

Despite what the oracle had foretold, the death of Paris and the possession of Heracles' weapons did not manage to make the Greeks victorious. Calchas then gave the Greeks more wisdom, telling them that only Helenus, the Trojan seer and prince, knew how to defeat Troy. Odysseus took the advice, and proceeded to capture Helenus on Mount Ida. Helenus bore a personal grudge against Troy. Helenus instructed the Greek leaders what to do in order to defeat Troy. First, the Greeks needed to bring Pelops' bones back to Asia, from Greece. Agamemnon accomplished this task. Secondly, they needed to bring Achilles' son Neoptolemus into the war, and so a group of Greeks travelled to Scyros to fetch him. Third, the Greeks were instructed to steal the Palladium, a sacred image of Athena, located in the goddess's temple in Troy. Diomedes and Odysseus took it upon themselves to complete this dangerous mission. Once they were inside the walls of Troy, Odysseus was recognized by Helen, who saw through his disguise but did not give him away. The two heroes seized the sacred image of Athena and escaped unscathed.

The famous Trojan horse then entered the story. Under Greek supervision, a great wooden horse was constructed. Unbeknownst to the Trojans, the horse construction had a hollow belly, which was big enough to hide several soldiers inside. One night, this horse was brought to the Trojan plain. Several Greek warriors climbed in to the belly of the horse, under Odysseus' direction. The remaining Greeks burned their camps and sailed off to wait at the nearby island of Tenedos.

The following morning, the Trojans were confused by the fact that the Greeks had gone, and instead, a huge, mysterious horse sat out the front of Troy. The Trojans also came across a Greek who remained, named Sinon, whom they took as prisoner. Sinon had been instructed by Odysseus to stay and be captured, and had been supplied with plausible stories about the Greek departure, the wooden horse, and his own reason for being there. Sinon told Priam and the other Troy soldiers that Athena had deserted the Greeks because of the theft of the Palladium. Without her help they had no hope, and decided to flee to avoid defeat. But in order to return home safely, they needed a human sacrifice. Sinon told them that he was chosen as the sacrifice, but managed to escape and hide. The horse had been left by the Greeks to placate the angry goddess, with the hope that the Trojans would desecrate it, earning Athena's hatred. These lies were believed by Priam and many other Trojans. However, Cassandra and a priest named Laocöon predicted that the horse was full of soldiers. These predictions were not believed. Laöcoon proceeded to hurl a spear at the horse, and in response a hostile God sent two large snakes to strangle him and his sons. The Trojans needed no further proof: they drew the gigantic horse inside their city gates to honor Athena.

That night, the soldiers crept from the horse, killing the sentries. They then opened the gates to let the Greek army in. The Greeks returned in the night, and set fires throughout the city. They massacred and looted the city. Once the Greeks were inside the walls, The Trojan resistance was no match. King Priam was slain by Neoptolemus, and by morning all but a few Trojans were dead. Of Trojan males, only Aeneas, with his father and son, had escaped the battle. Hector's young son Astyanax was thrown to his death from the walls of the city. The Princess Polyxena, whom Achilles had loved, was sacrificed brutally upon his tomb. Troy was devastated, and finally, Hera and Athena had exacted their revenge upon Paris and his city.

Now victorious in overthrowing Troy, the Greeks were now faced with the challenge of returning back to their various kingdoms. This was not to be an easy task, as the Gods had scores to settle with many Greek soldiers. Soon after the Greeks set sail, a powerful storm arose that blew much of the Greek fleet far off course.

Of those who travelled by ship, Agamemnon was one of the few that escaped the storm and reached home safely and with ease. During his absence however, his wife Clytemnestra had found a new lover, Aegisthus. Upon his return, they murdered him and his followers, including Cassandra, at the banquet table. Clytemnestra was hateful, and had never forgiven her husband for sacrificing Iphigenia.

Menelaus had planned to murder Helen when he found her in Troy, but upon seeing her naked breasts once again, he lost his motivation, and took her again as his wife. This offended Athena, and Menelaus and Helen and as a result were caught in the storm. They lost most of their ships, which were blown to Crete and Egypt. Unable to return to Sparta because of the winds, Menelaus settled in the new land, and began trading. Eight years later, the prophetic sea god Proteus, master of changes, gave him the secret to getting home safely. Also having had propitiated Athena, Menelaus was allowed to sail to Sparta with Helen, returning a rich man. Upon their eventual deaths, the pair went to the Isles of the Blessed, as favored relations of Zeus.

The surviving, and less-respected Ajax, who had raped Cassandra in the temple of Athena while plundering Troy, was shipwrecked on his way home. He survived the wreck, and made his way onto the rocks, where he celebrated having escaped the wrath of the gods. Poseidon saw this, and split the rock to which he clung, drowning him.

Nauplius resented most of the Greeks, and caused many of their ships to be destroyed on the Euboean coast by lighting a deceptive beacon. Philoctetes also held a grudge against the Greeks for his mistreatment. He chose to sail to Italy instead, where he founded two cities.

Achilles' son Neoptolemus followed in his father's footsteps, making himself known as a valiant fighter during the battle of Troy. Warned against ruling his home kingdom, he travelled instead to Epirus, where he became the Molossian King. Neoptolemus later travelled to Delphi where he demanded retribution from Apollo, for helping to kill his father. The priestess refused his request, and so he retaliated by robbing and burning the temple. He later returned again to Delphi, where he was killed in a dispute over sacrificial meat. Apollo's devotees then erected a new temple over his grave.

Of all the Greek soldiers, only the wise Nestor swiftly sailed home. He lived the rest of his life there amongst his sons, enjoying the fruits of old age in peace.

Chapter 12: Other Mythological Stories

There is no dearth for mythological stories in the Greek pantheon. In this chapter, you will discover some additional Greek myths.

Creation of the Universe

It is said that there was only Chaos in the beginning of the Universe. From out of nowhere, Erebrus emerged next, followed by the Night. When Love was born next, it marked the beginning of order. Light emerged from Love, who was followed by Gaea, Mother Earth.

It is believed that the union of the Night and Erebrus resulted in the birth of Ether, the heavenly light and also to Day, which is known as the light of earth. It is also said that Night went on to create Fate, Doom, Death, Dreams, Sleep, and Nemesis.

In the meantime, Gaea gave birth to Uranus, who became the god of the sky. Eventually, Uranus became Gaea's husband. Their union resulted in the birth of the 12 Titans, 3 Cyclopes, and 3 Hecatoncheires. However, several stories indicate that Uranus was a terrible and cruel husband and father. It was said that he hated the Hecatoncheires and pushed them back into Gaea's womb. Offended by Uranus' actions, Gaea instigated her children to rebel against Uranus. All her children were afraid of revolting against Uranus, except Cronus.

Gaea and Cronus devised a plan to bring an end to Uranus' tyranny. When Uranus was lying with Gaea in the night, Cronus came out of nowhere and grabbed his father. He went on to castrate his father using the sickle forged by Gaea, and threw his genitals into the ocean. Before he departed, Uranus swore to punish Cronus and the other Titans. It is said that magical creatures like the Ash tree nymphs, giants, and the Erinyes were born from the blood of Uranus that got spilt on earth, as a result of the castration.

With Uranus out of the picture, Cronus banished the Hecatoncheires and the Cyclopes to the underworld. He married his sister Rhea, and began ruling the world. We have already learned of how he was afraid of being usurped and ended up swallowing his children as soon as they were born. Rhea managed to save the life of her sixth child, who turned out to be Zeus. Zeus rose in rebellion against his father and also saved his other siblings. This resulted in the war between the Olympians and Titans. The Olympians won the war and the Titans were banished to the underworld.

Creation of Man

We know that Prometheus and Epimetheus sided with the Olympians during the war between the Titans and the Olympians. As a result, they were spared from Zeus' wrath. The brothers were tasked with the responsibility of creating world's first man. Prometheus shaped world's first man out of mud. Once the clay figurine was completed by Prometheus, Athena brought the figure to life.

Epimetheus was tasked with the responsibility of assigning different traits to the various creatures. As already mentioned, Epimetheus had given all the positive traits to animals and did not have any to assign to mankind. To compensate for this, Prometheus decided that men would stand on their feet, just like the gods. He also decided to gift mankind with fire.

Amalthea's horn

After giving birth to Zeus, Rhea hid him in a cave. This was to ensure that Zeus was not found by Cronus and ultimately swallowed by him, a fate met by Zeus' siblings. When Zeus was on the island, he was nursed and nourished by a goat called Amalthea. When Zeus was young, he was playing with Amalthea one day. While playing, he broke her horn accidentally. Filled with guilt as well as gratitude for Amalthea, Zeus blessed her horn. Accordingly, its owner would be able to find whatever they desired for, with the help of the horn. This was known as the horn of the Amalthea or the Cornucopia, which symbolized eternal abundance. When Amalthea died, her hide was used by Zeus to forge his thunder shield, Aegis.

Ages of Man

Greek myths suggest that mankind went through different eras, which were marked by specific events. These eras were known as the ages of man. According to a Greek poet, Hesiod, there were five ages of man. On the other hand, Ovid, a Roman poet, suggested that there were only four ages.

The five ages of man, according to Hesiod, were as follows:

Golden Age

In this Age, Cronus was ruling the world. It is said that mankind lived in harmony and constantly interacted with the gods. The golden age was marked by an abundance of produce and food, provided by nature. Because of the abundant resources, there was no need for humans to work. Devoid of manual labor, humans lived for a long time and their deaths happened in a peaceful manner.

Silver Age

During this age, the ruler of the world was Zeus. In this era, children would go on to live for a hundred years, under the protection of their mothers. As they aged and grew up, their lifespan was reduced. This could be attributed to the frequent clashes between mankind at this time. During this age, the humans did not pay any kind of offerings or tributes to the gods. Zeus killed most of the humans for this very reason.

Bronze Age

During this age, it is believed that men were tough and trained for warfare. Bronze was used by humans to not just create their weapons but also for their abodes. They constantly were engaged in war and often killed each other. The great flood of Deucalion marked the end of this Age.

Heroic Age

This era was not considered by Ovid. This age was considered as an improvement after all the discord in the silver and bronze ages. This was the time when the heroes and demigods existed. There are several stories about the heroes of this age and their brave deeds.

Iron Age

According to Hesiod, this was the age where he and his contemporaries lived in. This era was marked by destruction, desolation and pain. Humans would continue to fight with each other often and lose their peace in the process. They would remain selfish and would care only about their own interests. In the absence of indignation and shame, mankind would continue to destroy each other. It is also said that the gods abandoned the humans during this age.

As per Ovid, there was no heroic age. In his version, people living in the Golden age were not able to travel and explore the different parts of the world. Along with the Silver age came seasonal changes, which were brought about by Jupiter (who was the Roman equivalent of Zeus). It was during this age when man was gifted with agriculture too. The Bronze Age was characterized by warfare and humans killing each other. The Iron Age was also marked by warfare. Added to it, mankind also lacked loyalty and were not pious at all.

Conclusion

Thanks again for taking the time to read this book! I hope that you enjoyed learning about Greek mythology!

If you enjoyed this book, please take the time to leave me a review on Amazon. I appreciate your honest feedback, and it really helps me to continue producing high quality books.

CPSIA information can be obtained
at www.ICGtesting.com
Printed in the USA
LVHW082159200621
690729LV00011B/687